LITTLE PALACES

house and home in the inter-war suburbs

PUBLISHED BY MIDDLESEX UNIVERSITY PRESS

CONTENTS

Foreword   3
Sir Christopher Frayling

Preface   5
Lesley Hoskins

Introduction   7
Mark Pinney

Architecture   15
Mark Pinney

Decoration   31
Mark Turner

Household Management   43
Phillippa Mapes

Leisure   55
Sue Andrew

Transport   67
Malcolm Barres-Baker

References   81

Selected reading   82

Acknowledgements   83

MoDA   84

FOREWORD

This little book has a big purpose: to save the suburban house, and its inhabitants, from the enormous condescension of history. Virginia Woolf is reputed to have said that if she had to choose between death and living in Richmond, she would choose death; certainly, to Bloomsbury intellectuals the word 'suburban' was synonymous with much of what they despised about the modern world: bogus architectural styles, a bit of garden for the weekend, 'merrie Englandism', people who were unfashionable out-of-towners, the antithesis of life in 'society' and of Oxbridge intellectual fellowship. Most architects and writers on design in the inter-war years of the 20th century tended to agree with them. The only historical style they rated was Georgian – the geometry, the uniformity and the neo-classicism appealed to their modernist prejudices – and neo-Georgian was the least popular of suburban styles, partly because it was associated with London council housing and civic buildings.

Preferred architectural styles were 'Arts and Crafts' and 'Tudorbethan', with half-timbering stuck on the front, mullioned windows and a porch – all too easy to mock. If one of the great attractions of the suburban house was privacy, then the mini manor house with metaphorical drawbridge symbolised the fact. So it is appropriate that one of the great evocations of this kind of suburban lifestyle is the early chapters of JRR Tolkien's *Lord of the Rings* trilogy. The hobbits live in a ribbon-development village, garden gnomes come to life. They don't like the soot-black industrial city at all. From the early 1930s, streamlined white 'moderne' houses became fashionable in the suburbs as well, provided there was a slope in the roof. Flat roofs were all very well in Bauhaus theory but in English winters they tended to leak.

And then there was the iron sunburst on the gate. It is difficult to recover today just how innovative the suburban house was in the years following the First World War. The boom years were made possible by local authority building on a grand scale (remember that?), an obsession with dispersal (Dickensian cities were very unhealthy places), the availability of credit, loose planning controls, a vibrant specialist building sector and, above all, the realisation that people really did want to live in their own homes with their own front doors and back gardens – not in terraces, but in semi-detached or detached houses. The sunburst seemed to herald a new dawn.

I grew up in a brick-built detached house in South London, which is why, for me, the word 'suburban' has always been a term of endearment rather than a put-down. It is also why I warmly welcome *Little Palaces*. The book was, and is, a pioneering study of the suburban house – its look, its social context, its meaning. Not a nostalgic study, but a dispassionate and timely one. Even the architects are now beginning to catch on.

Sir Christopher Frayling
April 2003

PREFACE

Little Palaces was first published in 1987 to accompany an exhibition of the same name. Based on research done at the Silver Studio Collection (now the Museum of Domestic Design & Architecture, Middlesex University) by the then Keeper, Mark Turner, and his colleagues, it illustrated and described the architecture, the decoration and the way of life associated with the suburban semi-detached North London house of the 1920s and 30s.

At that time very little sympathetic attention had ever been paid to such homes, in spite of the fact that they had provided, and still do provide, the setting for a way of life that suits large numbers of families in this country.

Almost three million such houses were built in the inter-war period but the mainstream architectural press of the time was generally hostile. With a few exceptions, subsequent histories tended to ignore or deride semi-detached suburbia despite it having been a major social and architectural phenomenon. The result was that few people were interested in understanding these houses.

The situation is very different now, partly due to the original *Little Palaces*. Many people are fascinated by the social, architectural and decorative history of homes of all kinds and of all periods. Most conservationists and architectural historians have come to appreciate the once despised suburban areas of London; the inter-war 'semi' is recognised as having its own character and landscape, both worthy of preservation.

Nonetheless, the majority of individual houses have been, and are still being, updated - 'period' front doors, aluminium-framed double-glazing, artificial stone-cladding and front gardens paved for parking are the most usual alterations. The suburban environment has changed too. London Transport's far-reaching modernisation of its tube stations radically compromises their architectural coherence. The red telephone box, a characteristic component of the inter-war landscape, has all but disappeared. Many suburban buildings, such as churches and cinemas, are losing their original functions and being threatened with destruction.

For some this is an outrage. But it can also be argued that these improvements provide the individuality, comfort, convenience and modernity that are, and always have been, the essence of the suburban life.

This new edition is a timely contribution to the debate. With few changes to the text but a number of new illustrations, *Little Palaces* is once again available as a valuable resource for the understanding of the inter-war semi-detached house and its surroundings.

Lesley Hoskins
Curator
Museum of Domestic Design & Architecture
Middlesex University
2003

INTRODUCTION

'A House, a Home, a Little Palace, in a convenient healthy district, purchasable by anyone with a small capital and regular income…'

The idea of the suburban home was by no means new when John Laing & Son advertised their 'Little Palaces' at Colindale in 1930, for London's suburban growth had continued unabated since the early 19th century. However, the years 1919 – 1939 saw the suburban house achieve what still seems to be its most characteristic and widespread form, that of the small semi-detached villa with its own front door and garden, seemingly close to the countryside and yet within reach of shops, amenities and places of work. Unplanned and unfashionable, apparently without social or aesthetic virtue, it nonetheless represents the way in which perhaps the majority of people in this country wish to live.

For the impulse to live in the suburbs is deep-rooted; at its heart lies a rejection of life in the industrial city and a belief, in the words of the

New Ideal Homesteads Ltd brochure, about 1935. The company was a very big provider of houses for the lower end of the market. This type of house was available on all of their twenty estates in the London area.
BADDA 460

"K" TYPE from 14/4 WEEKLY £575 FREEHOLD

German writer on the English house, Hermann Muthesius, 'that to live in a private house is in every way a higher form of life'. In these years, this idea became attainable to greater numbers of people than ever before – and perhaps since – and in its pursuit vast areas around London were transformed. The countryside of Middlesex all but disappeared beneath a tide of houses, shopping parades, cinemas and by-pass roads. These districts acquired a way of life and a spirit of place that were new and distinct from other parts of London. In their turn, these now seem to have vanished.

In 1919, however, the picture was very different. The country faced a severe housing crisis for, in addition to existing shortages and inadequacies in the housing stock, building activity had virtually ceased for the duration of the First World War (1914-1918). The problem was to be met in a variety of ways but the most important consequence initially was that, for

The North Circular Road at Palmers Green, about 1935.

the first time, the state became a major provider of houses. The possible consequences of millions of servicemen returning from the trenches to dire conditions at home were found by the government to be sufficiently alarming (with the revolutions in Russia and later Germany in mind) to prompt a major campaign of local authority building. This was funded by the Treasury under the Addison Acts of 1919 and it acquired the slogan 'Homes Fit for Heroes'.

In London, guided by the Tudor Walters Report of 1918, these housing schemes continued the far-sighted work of the London County Council's (LCC's) housing department in taking the form of cottage estates in the outer suburbs, an example being the post-war section of the LCC's White Hart Lane estate at Tottenham. But in 1921 it was found expedient to terminate the campaign, with only 214,000 houses built nationally out of a projected 500,000. One of the casualties was the ambitious 1922 scheme to the north of Pymmes Park in Edmonton which, deprived of its subsidies, was drastically curtailed. In 1922 the Health Minister hoped that 'future state invention will not be required, and that building industry will return to its pre-war economic basis'; henceforth, the provision of houses was principally to be work of private enterprise.

In spite of subsidies extended by the government to private builders, building activity remained hampered by the high cost of materials for some years after the war and house prices were generally high. For many people, other solutions had to be sought. Shanty towns for the poor and unemployed grew around London, including one at Hendon. 'Plot lands' appeared in the surrounding countryside. People bought plots and erected their own dwellings, whether self-built or one of the prefabricated shacks and bungalows that were available. Railway carriages, caravans and houseboats were pressed into service and became rather fashionable in

time. But for those who could afford one, a speculatively built villa was
desirable and, in the absence of effective planning controls and with
farmers eager to sell land in the agricultural depression, it might be
situated on the South Downs or on a magnificent stretch of the coast.
Failing this, it could be in the fast-disappearing countryside of Middlesex or
Surrey, close to a new tube station or on an arterial road.

By the late 1920s, this prospect was brought within the reach of
greatly increased numbers of people. In 1922, 4,860 private homes were
built in Greater London, compared with 12,047 local authority ones. By
1925, following the withdrawal of the Addison subsidies, this had risen to
19,655 private houses, against only 3,826 council houses. Thereafter, council
housing levelled at about eight thousand to twelve thousand a year, while
private building climbed spectacularly, if erratically, to a peak of 72,756 in
1934.[1] This enormous increase in the numbers of privately built houses –
most of which were for sale rather than rent, unlike the majority of pre-
1914 houses – was possible because of the existence of a new class of
people able to buy their houses for the first time. The middle classes
emerged from the First World War both greater in number and poorer in
wealth than in 1914. Their ranks had been swollen by lower paid 'white
collar' workers in new administrative, clerical and retail occupations, while
the traditional, wealthier middle class had suffered a decline through
increased taxation and war-induced inflation. The new middle class was as
anxious as its predecessors to demonstrate its independence from the
urban working class by occupying a house in the suburbs – and was,
moreover, through the diversity of its occupations, relatively unaffected by
the Depression – and builders soon found that, by catering for this lower
end of the market, they could build and sell smaller and cheaper houses in
greater numbers than before.

New Ideal Homesteads Ltd brochure, about 1935.

BADDA 460

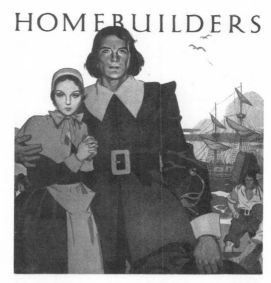

HOMEBUILDERS

NEW IDEAL
HOMESTEADS

Britain's Best and Biggest Builders.

The ability to buy houses was greatly extended in this period by the rapid growth of the building societies, who often worked together with builders. With mortgage repayments of as little as nine shillings a week, it became possible in the 1930s to buy a house on an income of less than £200 a year. New Ideal Homesteads were advertising their maisonettes in the mid 30s as, 'undoubtedly the cheapest form of homeowning…now within the reach of all earning £3 weekly or more', although a more representative instance might be repayments of fifteen shillings or a pound a week for a standard 'semi'. After the inflated period following the war, house prices fell in the late 1920s to well under £500 for the cheapest 'semis' and bungalows, with comfortable detached and semi-detached houses at between £750 and £1,500 and the top end of the market at around £2,000 to £2,500.

The creators of the suburbs were the speculative builders who ranged from large firms such as Davis and Laing, to local concerns of no more than four or five people putting up perhaps a single row of houses. Larger firms sometimes acted as developer and agent as well as builder, but a more common procedure was for the builder to buy plots of land parcelled out for building by a developer, such as George Cross of Edgware, and to rely on a local estate agent to dispose of the finished product. Since finance was usually borrowed from banks, it was necessary for houses to be built and sold as quickly as possible and speculative building was not always a predictable business. It helped to be able to anticipate the spread of development. Haymills, for example, began building in Hendon before the tube was extended there from Golders Green. Those who invested in land to the north of Edgware, in expectation of the tube extension to Bushey Heath authorised in 1937, lost money when it failed to materialise.

The provision of amenities in the suburbs was a somewhat random affair. Local authorities naturally played a role and the suburbs of Middlesex

Brochure for Davis Estates Ltd, about 1935.
BADDA 296

ESTATE DEVELOPMENT

contain a series of fine public buildings including libraries, swimming pools, town halls and schools, by the county's architect, WT Curtis. However, the suburbs were motivated above all by the essentially Victorian desire for a private family life and social and civic life took second place to this. In consequence, the suburbs rarely convey an impression of a communal entity and seldom attempt to create an effect of civic grandeur. Private enterprise occasionally filled the gap – cinemas flourished and Woodside Park, Finchley, for example, contained a sports club and social centre as part of its layout – but suburban recreation tended to be home-based. Collectivist instincts in general did not extend much beyond membership of a public library and the maintenance of an orderly front garden.

The proposed tube extension from Edgware seems to symbolise in a larger way the general termination of London's suburban growth, which occurred in 1939. Work on it began in 1939 and it was due for

completion in 1941, for it was assumed that London would simply go on growing outwards indefinitely. But work was suspended, never to be resumed, early in the Second World War (1939 -1945). Today at Mill Hill, Oakwood, Edgware and elsewhere, the houses stop and fields begin at the point where they did in 1939. This was foreshadowed by a drop in demand for houses from the mid 1930s, for the growing threat of aerial bombardment made many people reluctant to buy houses in the capital. But the real reason for the end to London's suburbia was the imposition of planning controls, notably the Town and Country Planning Act of 1947, before building could resume after the war. The unplanned sprawl of the suburbs represented everything the new breed of planning abhorred and after 1945 new building was either squeezed into existing development or banished to the new towns beyond the Green Belt.

Mark Pinney

ARCHITECTURE

Most suburban houses of the 1920s and 1930s were built without need of architect or planner, by speculative builders whose intention was to produce something that would sell for a profit. Partly for this reason, the inter-war suburban house has traditionally been the object of scorn among most writers on architecture and members of the architectural profession. As the houses went up, abuse was heaped upon them; they were despised for their use of – to use a vogue word of the period – 'bogus' architectural styles and deplored for their waste of the countryside. One voice which was rarely heard in this was that of the people who chose to live in them. 'The people in these places are all alike', was one view expressed.[1] And yet it is clear from the immense, unspoken popularity of these houses that they expressed the tastes and aspirations which drove thousands of

The New Estates Magazine, 1934, issued by E&L Berg Ltd. Berg was an important developer in the Surrey area. As well as traditionally styled houses they offered the modern 'Sunspan' home, designed by Wells Coates and Pleydell Bouverie.
BADDA 457

Hendon Heights Estate, Hendon, as shown in a Haymills brochure of the 1920s. These substantial houses have the trademark features of inter-war suburban homes – lead lights, tile-hanging and half-timbering.

people in the 20s and 30s to move out to the new suburbs and, in most cases, to own a house for the first time. Fortunately, it is at last becoming recognised that they have histories and qualities of their own that are worthy of affection and respect.

THE SUBURBAN VILLA

A London suburban house of the 1920s and 1930s might be detached, semi-detached or part of a small terrace. In all cases, however, its front door would be approached through a front garden, however small, with a larger garden at the rear and perhaps a planted verge by the road. It would probably be part of a row of similar houses but the road might curve to break up the row and closer inspection would reveal subtle differences between one house and the next. Its facade might display decorative features derived from English vernacular architecture such as tile-hanging and half-timbering and these rural associations could be elaborated in stained-glass landscapes over the front door. In most cases it would try to appear welcoming rather than imposing, evoking the countryside rather than the metropolis.

This picture of the English suburban house is now so familiar that it is sometimes difficult to remember that it once seemed strikingly different from the sorts of houses lived in by most people. The cost of building and the need, with transport systems only partially developed, to remain close to places of work had made it necessary for the majority of 19th century houses to be built in high densities in terraces. Although increasing efforts were made to emphasise the individual house by means of features such as porches, gables and bay windows, the terraces were often built in straight, parallel rows with little room for gardens. The materials of the London terraced house were uniform: stock bricks – usually brown, turning black in the coal smoke, though with red ones later used for frontages – with slate roofs and some ornamental stucco and cast iron. Houses were deep, with narrow frontages allowing little access for light and air, which were further restricted by the frequent extension at the rear.

By contrast, the wealthier classes tended to pursue the fashionable habit established early in the 19th century of imitating country life by living in a house situated in a salubrious, leafy district further out. This house would be detached and secluded behind generous plantings and, after the 1870s, would probably be in the neo-vernacular 'Queen Anne' style. Clearly, by the end of the century, confidence in the terraced street as the most urbane form of housing had been lost and it all too often seemed gloomy, monotonous, unhealthy and cramped.

Typical turn-of-the-century suburban houses in Palmers Green. Photographed in the 1920s.

A well-planned estate of substantial houses at the Meadway in Southgate, built by Messrs Edmonsons Ltd. Photographed in the late 1920s.

In 1898, a radical alternative was proposed in Ebenezer Howard's book, familiar under its later title, *Garden Cities of Tomorrow*. The Garden City Movement envisaged new communities of houses in the countryside, surrounded by greenery but grouped around new industries and amenities. Howard's ideas were put into practice by the architect and planner Raymond Unwin at Letchworth (begun 1903) and its successors. In contrast to the pattern of 19th-century town housing, Unwin built houses that were semi-detached or in short terraces, had their own large gardens and were laid out in winding roads or cul-de-sacs or grouped around greens. By planning in this way, Unwin reduced costly road frontages and made it economically possible to build in low densities. Architecturally, the houses were in the plain but picturesque cottage-vernacular idiom then current among progressive architects.

The Garden City Movement had a social, reformatory purpose but its lessons were not lost on the speculative builder, who did no more than offer an escape from the city for those able to afford it. Its principles were also applied, in a rather more thorough manner, to state housing after World War One in the beautifully designed suburban cottage estates; indeed, it signalled the acceptance generally of the low-density suburb as the ideal means of housing the population.

Its most immediate effect on the speculative suburban house was the widespread abandonment of the terrace in favour of the detached or semi-detached house. For example, Haymills Ltd, in Golders Green, were building even quite expensive houses in terraces before 1914 but built only detached houses after the war. This was possible because, for social reasons, the post-war house was smaller than its predecessor and therefore cheaper to build. Other Garden City principles, though, were less fully assimilated. The plan of most suburban houses, for instance, remained extremely conservative; in fact, in most cases it was essentially the same as that of the 19th-century terraced house. The entrance hall and staircase would be on one side, with a front parlour and rear dining room on the other. The kitchen would be at the rear with the bathroom and two or more bedrooms above. Unwin's attempt to reform this plan by removing the parlour, which he considered both unnecessary and undesirable, met with great resistance and few suburban houses were without one. However, speculative builders followed Unwin in removing the rear

This is a plan for a relatively large house but it has a typical layout. From The Bride's Home, *about 1935.*
BADDA 319

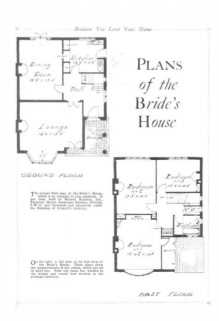

An aerial view of suburban development in Enfield in about 1935.

extension, an unpopular if useful device, and had in consequence to reduce the size of the kitchen and bathroom. The frontages of houses were also generally widened somewhat to admit more light and air and to allow direct access to the garden from the rear reception room. But the houses themselves still tended to be built in rather straight, dense rows. Builders, especially smaller ones working with small, awkwardly-shaped plots, still found it hard to resist fitting in as many houses as possible.

Greater efforts in this direction were made in the 1930s, with Laing laying out their estates from 1930 in a way that preserved existing trees and followed the natural contours of the ground. Their 1939 Broadfields Avenue Estate, Edgware, was planned in concentric rings and had wide planted verges. Advertisements began to claim low densities, as at FJC Ingram's Woodside Park Estate, Finchley, which had 'not more than eight houses per acre', while estates were frequently described as 'garden suburbs', justifiably or not, such as R and E Davis's 'Stanmore Garden Suburb', Brockley Avenue of 1936. This may have been due to an awareness of the criticism of the speculative builder which had been growing throughout the 20s and 30s. The architectural profession resented the fact that so many houses could be built without its involvement and considered that architects were required to 'improve' the standard of design and planning, which they considered lamentably low. Competitions were held by the Architectural Association and the Gidea Park Estate in the early 1930s to find architects' designs for suburban houses, while the Royal Institute of

British Architects reduced its fees for speculative work to encourage builders to employ its members.[2] A growing number of architects (though few notable ones) began to work for builders but, as the RIBA's journal had to point out, the efforts of an architect did not always make a house more attractive in the eyes of a purchaser; indeed, quite the reverse, as builders could find to their cost.[3] The problem of the gap between the tastes of architects and that of ordinary people remained unresolved.

SUBURBAN STYLES

Although inter-war architecture is often seen only in terms of the emergence of the Modern Movement and the development of 'moderne' or 'modernistic' derivatives, it is in fact marked by an astonishing diversity of styles. Nowhere is this more true than in the case of speculative housing; indeed it is by no means uncommon to see a row of suburban houses by the same builder, each of which is in a different style from its neighbour. *Ideal Home* magazine contained a feature in the 1920s, illustrating pairs of houses identical in plan but quite different in styles, and it was usual for suburban estates to contain houses in a selection of styles such as 'Tudor', 'Georgian', or 'Modern' (ie neo-vernacular). This tendency became more marked from the early 1930s when builders threatened to oversupply the market with houses and something eye-catchingly different was required to tempt the public. Moderne styles were experimented with and ever more extravagant advertising claims made for 'Super Houses', 'Sunshine Houses' and 'Hollywood Homes'. However, most house buyers remained conservative in their architectural preferences and few builders were prepared to risk their sales by introducing anything radically new.

The most common form of the inter-war suburban house derived from the great revival of English domestic architecture which had taken place during the late Victorian and Edwardian periods. Architects such as

Richard Norman Shaw, Sir Edwin Lutyens and CFA Voysey had used the elements of rural-vernacular architecture to create a type of house that was to be immensely influential and attractive, especially among the middle classes whose wealth came from towns and to whom it supplied a note of rural nostalgia. Its natural home therefore was perhaps in the suburbs and, after 1918, speculative builders began to apply its features en masse to the ordinary semi-detached house.

A cheaper house of this sort would typically be asymmetrical, with a projecting bay running through both storeys up to a gable on one side, and the front door and porch under a steeply pitched roof on the other. Materials would be varied; red facing bricks were relieved with pebbledash or hung tiles, while the roof would have rather bright tiles. Nailed planks imitating half-timbering might adorn the gable and in many cases the windows would have leaded panes.

Woodwork would be brightly painted in contrasting colours – Brunswick green and cream, chocolate brown and pale yellow – or

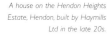

A house on the Hendon Heights Estate, Hendon, built by Haymills Ltd in the late 20s.

perhaps brush-grained to imitate oak. Its general aspect would no doubt seem crowded and restless to an architectural eye, with little of the wall plane allowed to show beneath the 'features'; and yet it tried and succeeded in creating, as far as cost would allow, an impression of welcoming, 'cottagey'. charm.

More expensive examples, of course, could aspire more closely to the ideals of the vernacular revival. For example, AJ Reynolds' mid-30s 'Tudor Grange' house (£3,500) on the Manor Hall Estate, Hendon, had 'multi-coloured bricks and tile-hanging, relieved with oak half-timbering. There is a Stone Porch (with Gothic Head) to the front entrance, and generally an air of an English Country House', while the 'Wentworth' house (£2,750) was 'deliberately treated with Rustic Facing Bricks and Tiles to give the impression of maturity'. The ideals of age and tradition were sought: CWB Simmonds' Cedars Close Estate of c1930 (architect HW Binns), built in the grounds of Hendon Hill, was 'on historic land, well matured…There is nothing new about it except the houses'.

However, the ultimate expression of the confused, conservative romanticism of the suburbs was the neo-Tudor style. For many home buyers their 'dream house' was a fantasy of ancient timbering and thatched roof concealing a wealth of stained and polished oak. Pushing back the

secure front door, the owner would enter a dark, spacious hall to be greeted by a welcoming hearth with cosy inglenook, while a bay window framed with wisteria looked out to a garden filled with roses. Such houses filled the pages of *Ideal Home* and PA Barron's book, *The House Desirable*, of 1929, which illustrated extraordinary neo-Tudor houses by architects such as Blunden Shadbolt. These incorporated authentic timbers taken from demolished buildings and even reproduced sagging rooflines. Somewhat different, though equally curious, were the thatched and timber-framed houses built by Ernest Trobridge in north-west London in the 1920s.

Barron's ideal was of a 'hand built' house tailored to an individual client like a suit of clothes but most speculative houses are bought, as it were, off-the-peg, so most suburban Tudorists had to be content with 'Tudorbethan' details stuck on to ordinary semi-detached houses. Arthur Curton built great numbers of this sort of house in Edgware from 1927, while larger detached examples can be found on Edmonsons' Meadway Estate at Southgate. Nonetheless, even the cheaper examples succeeded in creating a compelling image of secure domesticity in a troubled age. The critic Anthony Bertram was perhaps right in 1938 to diagnose 'the popular love for the Tudor, whether bogus or genuine' as the result of a 'wish to escape…These are insecure and frightening times and I believe that economic depression and the fear of war are the chief promoters of the Tudoresque'.[4]

The undisguised fakery and at times dream-like fantasy of the neo-Tudor house placed it beyond the bounds of 'acceptable' taste. Fashionable opinion between the wars generally favoured a revival of the Georgian style, a taste shared by most leading architects, including those of the LCC who designed the suburban cottage estates of the 1920s. Amid the privately-built suburbs, however, the style met with considerable resistance. This has usually been put down to snobbery on the part of the proud home owner who did not want his house to look like a council house. This was no doubt true but it was also the case that neo-Georgian was simply not liked by many suburbanites, whose architectural values were still essentially Victorian and to whom the plain, rectilinear Georgian style would have seemed wanting in ornament and colour. Furthermore, Georgian architecture was associated not merely with council housing but with the terraces of inner London, which at that date constituted the greater part of the city's slums.

If the style was to be acceptable, it was frequently necessary to adorn it with quantities of costly urns, balusters, 'Adam' porches and other classical trimmings and, as a result, neo-Georgian became confined largely to token representation on the more expensive estates. Occasionally a more sophisticated essay in the pared-down Georgian of architects like Oliver Hill was attempted, such as AJ Reynolds' 'Manor' house at Hendon; even this, however, eschewed the small-paned sash window, essential in giving rhythm and proportion to Georgian facades, in favour of leaded casements. Without such concessions to popular taste, builders could experience difficulty in persuading customers of the attractiveness of the style. FJC Ingram, for instance, had to assure prospective buyers that the somewhat austere 'Georgian' house on his Woodside Park Estate, Finchley, was 'definitely a period house' and 'undoubtedly delightful looking'.

While the speculative builder cultivated a preoccupation with a mythical past, an equally romantic view began to grow of the modern world. In the early 1930s, it became possible to find among the Tudor and vernacular creations of the suburbs a quite different kind of house, superficially at least: with white walls, flat roof and 'streamlined' forms, it evoked the latest developments in technology, such as ocean liners, aircraft and locomotives, to speak confidently of a benevolent future.

Haymills 'Moderne' houses in Ashley Lane, Hendon, designed by Herbert Welch. Photograph from a sales brochure of 1931-32.

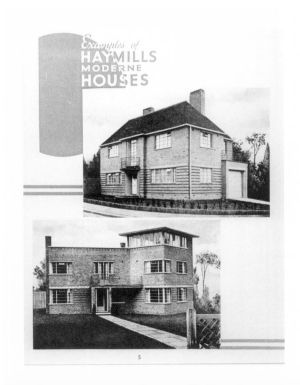

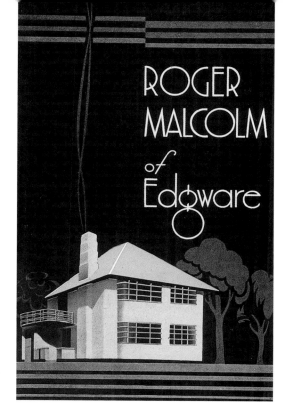

The graphic design of this brochure of about 1932 emphasises the modernity of Roger Malcolm's houses.
BADDA 311

These houses were partly a response to the continental Modern Movement which by 1930 had belatedly found adherents in this country. The Modernists asserted that society had entered a new era in which all existing architectural styles were obsolete and which demanded a totally new method of building based on industrialised materials and techniques. This notion was of course meaningless to the ordinary house buyer but the new style had sufficient novelty value to be taken up in the rather cautious form introduced at the Crittall window company's model village at Silver End, Essex, in the 1920s. One of the pioneers was Haymills, who in 1931-32 erected several white-walled, flat-roofed moderne houses at Ashley Lane, Hendon to the designs of their new consultant architect, Herbert Welch. They were not a popular success, despite being 'launched with much publicity and a briefing of the technical press who, regrettably, showed no more interest than the public in this new departure. The logic of the flat roof…did not appeal, and the experiment lapsed'.[5] The public was suspicious of this foreign, conspicuously new style which had lately become the subject of satirical cartoons in the press. However, it appeared that a superficial layer of modernity was popular when applied to an otherwise soundly traditional house – modern but not, as one South Coast builder put it, 'bizarre or Continental'. In 1932, Welch designed a new type of house for the Edgware builder Roger Malcolm which employed white stuccoed walls, horizontal steel-framed windows and curved 'sun trap' bays on a conventional hipped-roof 'semi'. Malcolm was careful to point out that it was 'not contrived with the frigid austerity of geometrical *modernism*'. This design was evidently successful, for Basil Gordon at Edgware, Allen Fairhead at Southgate, as well as Haymills and other firms, were soon building very similar things.

The simultaneous appeal of the olde worlde and the moderne is characteristic of the confused and polarised 1930s but it is not as paradoxical as it might appear. For both modes seemed equally to reject the values of the industrial city and to proclaim that the inhabitants had left the grimly 19th-century streets for a life filled with light, comfort and health. The exoticism of the new style was often enhanced by motifs such as Spanish wrought iron and brilliantly glazed blue and green pantiles, which brought to mind Hollywood or the Mediterranean.

Sunshine, one of the decade's obsessions, became the catchword for these houses; indeed, Roger Malcolm seemed to promise a completely transformed climate with houses that were 'streaming with light, inviting the sun; where chill is impossible…where the protection against the vagaries of the English weather is complete'. Inevitably, the reality proved less alluring.

After a few English winters, the white stucco cracked and the metal window frames corroded; the sun all too often failed to shine on the sun roof and in many cases they were quickly roofed over to make an extra storey. Like all attempts at modernity, the 'Sunshine House' very soon looked dated and after 1935 the fashion for it faded away.

FLATS

England, unlike Scotland or many continental countries, had no tradition of living in flats. During the latter half of the 19th century, however, blocks of flats began to be built in London. At one end of the social scale were those erected by philanthropic bodies such as the Guinness and Peabody trusts and, after 1893, the LCC; and at the other, privately-built 'mansion blocks' for the well-off in the West End. In the 1930s, speculatively-built blocks of service flats began to appear in the outer suburbs. They favoured more expensive districts (Southgate, Golders Green and Hendon, for example) and were usually prominently sited on arterial roads or shopping parades. The attraction of the flat lay not in economy – for rents at £100 to £300 per annum compared unfavourably with mortgage repayments on a house – but in their convenience for those unwilling to undertake the running of a house. Some were meant to accommodate families but the majority were designed for single people, businessmen and professionals, whose families might live out of town. For this reason, advertisements made much of the 'labour saving' qualities of flats and they were usually equipped with the latest devices such as built-in kitchens, electric fires and central heating.

Many local builders built flats in addition to houses (for example, Mulberry Close, Hendon, by CWB Simmonds and Edgware Close, Hendon, by Reginald Streather). But the larger developments were often the work of big property companies such as Edgware Court, Edgware by Harold Samuel Properties of Mayfair. This was designed, like many such blocks, by a West End architectural firm, in this case Marshall and Tweedy, whose other work included Viceroy Court (1936) to the north of Regents Park. The architect's role in these cases was usually to apply a 'treatment' to the facades of otherwise utilitarian blocks, such as Gregory and Brosan's Vincent Court, Hendon of 1935, whose streamlined facade masks vast barrack-like blocks behind.

From films of the period, it would appear that the service flat was popularly held to epitomise modern living at its most sophisticated and luxurious. This was certainly the effect aimed at by most developers. Stylistically, suburban flats tended to emulate the blend of sleek neo-Georgian and extrovert moderne employed on the blocks that were transforming the West End in this period. Many were equipped with swimming pools and tennis courts. The fad for sunshine was not neglected – the modernistic Northwood Hall, Hornsey Lane, for example, had curved 'sun trap' windows in addition to the usual balconies. However, since this cosmopolitan image was likely to be somewhat unsavoury to many suburbanites, very different 'cottage flats' were occasionally offered, usually of only two or three storeys and in a homely vernacular style. Ernest Trobridge even produced half-timbered flats at Kingsbury – his 'Highfort' in Buck Lane is amongst his most romantic creations. But whatever its style, the speculative suburban flat was never presented as more than an alternative to the house; it was not envisaged, as the followers of the Modern Movement hoped, that it should supersede it.

Mark Pinney

DECORATION

From the late 19th century onwards, the growing middle classes of the suburbs had taken an enthusiastic interest in the decoration of their houses. Until the advent of World War One in 1914, the cost of most household goods had been falling in proportion to income (this was due to increasingly efficient mechanised production and ever-growing competition from abroad) so even the humblest could afford to change wallpapers from time to time, or buy new Nottingham lace curtains without fear of the bankruptcy court.

Although shortages of both labour and materials after World War One led to a steep increase in prices, this proved to be a temporary state of affairs and home decoration continued to be as popular as ever. It was during the aftermath of the war that two of the most popular and long-running home decoration journals first appeared: *Homes and Gardens* (1919) and *Ideal Home* (1920). The early issues of these magazines provide a clear insight into middle-class decoration tastes in the early years of the 1920s. Even today, some older people can recall the horrors of the sharp increase in income tax that reduced many genteel people to comparative poverty. For these, the newly poor, the magazines provided articles on how to supplement an ever-dwindling income by dog breeding and chicken farming.

Solutions to the housing crisis were provided in the form of tasteful conversions of dilapidated cottages. These magazines broke new ground by showing black and white photographs of interiors of houses owned by real, and often famous, people. Above all, they sang the praises of the old and antique. Tudor oak panelling, early Victorian chintzes, Persian rugs and Georgian furniture, all were juxtaposed to form that uniquely English decorating style, termed 'Stockbroker Tudor' by Osbert Lancaster. This was rather unjust of him, for modest English country houses had been decorated

Inexpensive furnishing fabrics in the popular
'autumn tints' of the 1930s. Illustrated in
Hawkin's Household Catalogue, 1933.
BADDA 72

More FURNISHING FABRICS

REVERSIBLE PRINTED CASEMENT.
A well-covered floral design. Available also
in ground shades of Brown, Black and two
shades of Fawn. 50 ins. wide. *The Ground Shade
illustrated above should be Green, not
Blue.* H.C. 761 Quality. Yard **1'1½**

DUPLEX PRINTED CRETONNE.
Charming Chrysanthemum design on a two-tone
background, printed on both sides. Also in
ground shades of Blue, Green, Black and three
shades of Fawn. 50 ins. wide.
H.C. 771 Quality. Yard **1'2½**

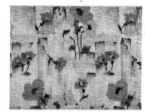

SHADOW TISSUE. A very charming
floral design. Available also in ground shades
of Blue, Green, Brown and two
shades of Fawn. 47/48 ins. wide.
H.C. 781 Quality. Yard **1'6½**

SHADOW TISSUE. In smart slub effect
with Poppies and Cornflower in two-tone
background forming a very attractive design.
Also in ground shades of Blue, Green and two
shades of Fawn. 30 ins. wide.
H.C. 791 Quality. Yard **1'0½**

PRINTED ART. SILK CASEMENT.
A charming floral and geometrical design
printed on an Art. Silk Brocade Casement.
All Cedar Grounds with flowers of Blue, Green,
Russet, Gold also Tangerine as
illustrated. 48 ins. wide.
Quality E.P.E. Yard **1'11**

FADELESS BROCADE CASEMENT. An
excellent fabric which drapes beautifully. Also
in Cedar, Gold, Golden Brown, Vieux Rose, Russet,
New Green and Blue. 31 ins. wide.
N.W.B. Quality. Yard **9½D.**
For other widths see page 17.

JOHN HAWKINS & SONS LTD., GREENBANK MILLS, PRESTON

Page 16

in much this way for decades. However, for many middle-class people it was,
and still is, seen to be the best way to do up one's house. During the 1920s
and 30s, many of the larger new suburban houses were photographed in
these magazines and most had adopted this charming and eclectic style.

In speculatively built suburbia, there was a very different way of decorating that had its roots firmly in the mid-Victorian taste. It is in 1920s interior decoration that we can see most clearly the huge gulf that existed between upper and lower middle-class taste. While smart suburban residents had cream distempered walls, Georgian furniture and oriental rugs, the residents of Edmonton and New Southgate had dark varnished wallpaper, cast-off Victorian furniture and linoleum. If one is fortunate enough to see an untouched semi-detached of the 1920s or 30s, the most striking feature to modern eyes is the overwhelming darkness of the interior. The ordinary suburban resident saw no particular merit in lightness in interior decoration. While there is no doubt that darkness was preferred for aesthetic reasons, there were strong practical reasons, too. Anyone who has attempted to live with open coal fires as the main means of heating will be only too aware of the vast quantities of dust to be dealt with each

A baronial setting for gas fires in this advert of the late 1920s.
SM 11

day. On light colours and textiles the effect is disastrous. If, on the other hand, one's woodwork is grained to imitate dark oak or is painted a rich chocolate brown, a daily deposit of soot only increases the darkness and at spring cleaning time, all is made as good as new with a coat of varnish.

Throughout the inter-war period, the majority of purchasers of speculatively- built houses were given very little choice in the initial decorative scheme. The exterior was almost invariably painted in two colours. There were many permutations and each builder seems to have had his own preference. Wates, for example, favoured Brunswick green and cream. Ideal Homesteads used chocolate brown and cream. Inside, all woodwork was either brush-grained (this was particularly favoured by the better quality builders such as Laing) or painted a stone colour to provide a suitable undercoat for subsequent graining. Ceilings were distempered

Gloss colours were mostly used for woodwork, kitchens and bathrooms. Flat (matt oil) colours were used mainly for walls. Robbialac paint chart of about 1920. SM 12

Late 1920s wallpaper. SW 434

white and bathrooms and kitchens given a coat of matt oil paint chosen from a limited colour range — typically cream, eau-de-Nil green or duck-egg blue. For other rooms, builders were prepared to offer a choice of wallpapers. Before World War Two (1939 -1945), most builders' merchants kept a stock of wallpapers made up from the products of the cheaper manufacturers such as Potters of Darwin and Lightbown & Aspinall. These cheap papers show perhaps better than anything the changes in popular taste during the 20s and 30s.

In the early 1920s, exotic wallpapers were fashionable. Imitation Chinese lacquer papers, with deep blue or red grounds, provided an ideal background for a tired housewife to enjoy Louise Miln's highly popular novels. (They were usually about an innocent English girl falling in love with a Chinese aristocrat.) The success of *The Sheik* (both the novel and the film) was responsible for endless desert scene wallpaper friezes, with camels, pyramids and palm trees. Above all, the discovery of the tomb of Tutenkhamun in 1922, ensured that Egyptian motifs remained one of the

Early 1930s wallpaper. SW 723

most popular forms of decoration right up until 1939. In the late 1920s, wallpapers which featured all-over leaf and berry motifs were the most popular, particularly for sitting and dining rooms. As the 30s progressed, modernistic designs of squares, chevrons and half circles, very loosely based on cubism, and usually softened by sprays of naturalistic or stylised flowers, became ubiquitous in lower middle-class suburbia.

Wallpapers show changes in fashionable colours with great accuracy. Bright reds, blues and greens in the early 1920s were replaced by softer greys, pinks and blues in the late 20s, but the 30s were dominated by 'autumn tints'. This was a universal expression for what was a uniquely English suburban range of colours: creams, oranges, browns, greens and reds. They were used for everything – carpets, linoleums, curtain fabrics and above all wallpapers. The 20s and 30s were also great decades for wallpaper friezes and borders. Small, stylised flowers in wonderfully rich colours were popular in the 20s and so were proper landscapes. 'The Mediterranean Coast by Moonlight', 'English Woodland in Springtime' and 'The Deserts of Arabia', were all highly popular subjects. In the 30s, friezes became bigger and more elaborate and often were very expensive. Many were based on trailing leaves and flowers and both Sanderson and John Line introduced borders to go above wainscot or skirting, so one could have a room papered to resemble a herbaceous border. If the border was an elaborate one, the wallpaper was usually plain buff or cream (porridge) colour and frequently embossed to provide an interesting texture.

Until the late 1930s it was customary, even in the cheapest of houses, to give all downstairs rooms a picture rail and the hall and dining room a dado rail as well. Below the dado rail a lincrusta, or more usually, an anaglypta paper was hung, brush-grained and varnished the same colour as the woodwork. Another mid-Victorian practice which survived in ordinary suburbia was to paint in two colours those internal doors which had not been grained. The framework was done in one colour and the panels in another. Red and yellow, brown and yellow, and green and cream were

Catesbys
ONE   PIECE
LINOLA
SQUARES

SIZE.			£	s.	d.
7ft. 6in. × 9ft. 0in.	...	1	8	6
9ft. 0in. × 9ft. 0in.	...	1	13	6
9ft. 0in. × 10ft. 6in.	...	1	19	6
9ft. 0in. × 12ft. 0in.	...	2	5	0
10ft. 6in. × 12ft. 0in.	...	2	15	0

DESIGN ILLUSTRATED is No. KL.680.
Other "LINOLA" designs post free;
write stating colour and size required.

popular. In rooms which received a lot of wear, such as halls and dining
rooms, varnished papers were used. These quickly went a very dark yellowish
brown and made the pattern and original colour quite undetectable.

After choosing the wallpapers, the owner of a new suburban house
would be obliged to choose something to cover the floorboards. For the
majority this inevitably meant linoleum. Most Londoners eventually made

their way to Catesby's on the Tottenham Court Road, for they had the best stock of linoleum. There were conventions to follow here. For halls, a pattern that imitated encaustic tiling or parquet flooring was preferred. Parquet patterns were also very popular for sitting rooms. In dining rooms, a reproduction of Turkey carpet was often used. In bedrooms, a wide range of copies of flowering Axminsters were available. One never used real carpeting in bedrooms, except for what were appropriately known as 'slip mats'. During the 1930s, lino was available in fashionable modernistic

This advertisement of about 1935 shows a good cross section of furnishing fabrics for the suburban house.

SM 10

patterns to go with the wallpaper. In the dining room and sitting room, a carpet square would be purchased if at all possible. This could be a traditional Axminster or, in the late 1930s, a cubist pattern in fashionable oranges, browns and greens.

The old-fashioned window treatment of Nottingham lace half-blinds, Venetian blinds and velvet, chenille or plush curtains that was considered suitable for 19th-century town houses, was not much adhered to in new suburban villas. The bay windows and leaded casements demanded a different treatment. Magazines recommended frilled valances and light casement curtains of cotton, silk or rayon. These could be left half-drawn to ensure daytime privacy without the expense of lace or muslin curtains. Cretonnes and chintzes were still widely used for both curtains and loose covers and tended to be based on designs similar to those of wallpaper. Loose covers were still very prevalent to protect upholstery from ravages of coal dust.

Furnishing the suburban semi was a difficult and expensive business. The upper middle-class habit of collecting antique furniture was not followed, possibly because old furniture was thought to be a sign of poverty or a potential source of dirt and bed bugs. Be that as it may, many

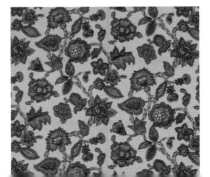

Mid-1930s printed cotton in a modern Jacobean style. This fabric would have been used for curtains.
ST 243

housewife. In addition, fashion in the 1930s demanded a return to the more feminine woman. Many women's magazines, such as *The Ladies Companion*, offered tips 'for the busy little housewife' at the same time as beauty columns suggesting 'hubby likes you to keep that girlish prettiness, you know'.[2] Furthermore, reports published in 1904 about the poor state of health of the British forces in the Boer War, blamed their condition on a neglected domestic environment. The home thus became of national importance, with schools beginning to provide lessons in domestic science. Since it was the school-children of this period who became the adults of the 20s and 30s, it is not surprising that the obsession with hygiene and cleanliness found its fullest expression in the inter-war years, with the responsibility for the state of the nation lying chiefly with wives and mothers. All these preoccupations were effectively focused on the new atmosphere of suburban life: the breadwinning husband returning to his healthy 'cottage in the country' and the cosy domesticity of his well-turned-out, neat wife and warm, clean home – all this made incongruously possible by the cold science and technology of the rapidly expanding domestic appliance industry.

HOUSEWORK AND THE APPLIANCE OF SCIENCE

The crucial feature which enabled the housewife to manage the servantless house was the development of electricity for home use. By 1890, coal and gas for cooking, heating and lighting had been exploited to their fullest extent. However, there was room for improvement of existing appliances. Electricity as a new form of power offered a wider scope and fresh possibilities; the magazine *Tit-Bits* in February 1926, even suggested that electricity would aid in the quest for hygiene to such an extent that a large percentage of babies born in 1940 would live to see 2040.[3] The gas and electricity companies fought each other fiercely in the inter-war period to win the approval of the housewife. Electricity's main disadvantage was its high price. In addition, people distrusted its powerful yet invisible qualities, whereas gas was already an established and trusted power source. In response, electricity companies tried to promote their product as 'The Good Fairy' – convenient, efficient and clean.[4]

However, with the establishment of the Central Electricity Board in 1926 (bringing some order to the differences in price and supply of London's many generating companies), the cost of electricity in the inter-war period steadily fell, while the real prices of coal and gas stayed more or less the same.[5] The benefits of electricity thus became obvious and universal in virtually all the new North London suburban houses. With the new availability of labour-saving appliances, and the increase in the amount of housework to be done without the aid of servants, it became necessary to redesign the kitchen itself. Previously the domain of the resident maid, the Victorian kitchen was large, often with a cast iron range for cooking, heating and hot water. It was often regarded as a monster, demanding constant cleaning, black leading and attention. A complex of adjoining rooms led off the kitchen – a scullery for washing, a coal shed and a larder.

Now that the lady of the house was obliged to spend more time in the kitchen, with or without the help of a 'daily', emphasis lay on lightness, cleanliness and convenience. Cooker, sink and worktops were 'scientifically' arranged in one room to minimise movement and effort, and the open-shelved dresser was replaced by the more hygienic fitted cupboard. The installation of an independent boiler made hot water more easily obtainable. For those living in the Edwardian suburbs of North London, these new demands meant extensive renovations. But owners of houses built in the 1920s and 30s could delight in the new 'kitchenette', a room often as small as ten feet by six feet, justified on labour-saving grounds but constructed by builders primarily to save space.

Advertisement for a domestic boiler to provide constant hot water, from Good Housekeeping, *June 1930.*

For less affluent families in the new suburbs, mortgage repayments restricted the purchase of household appliances. As one resident of Palmers Green in the 1930s recalled, there was only sufficient income left for 'kippers and curtains', although the availability of domestic equipment sold on 'easy terms' or hire purchase enabled many to take advantage of the rapidly expanding appliance industries. These industries, which boomed during the Depression, were quick to react to the incentive of home ownership and increased purchasing power of its customers. Cleanliness and economy of time and effort became marketable forces. This was evident in gas and electric cooker designs; previously constructed for hire by ironfounders, these had been built to last. With the facility for purchase, emphasis lay not on durability but on appearance and price. Cookers were now made largely of pressed steel panels covered in easy-to-clean enamel of black, white or mottled grey. Perhaps the greatest technical development in the design of gas stoves was the introduction of the 'Regulo' thermostat control in 1923. This ensured an even oven temperature without constant checking, so enabling the cook to carry out other tasks in the meantime. It was this advantage, as well as a cheaper price, that ensured the popularity of gas cookers over electric. Electricity triumphed, however, for lighting and in its capacity to power small appliances such as toasters and kettles. Belling & Co Ltd of Enfield offered an electric boiling ring for nineteen shillings (95p) 'with innumerable uses which are by no means restricted to the kitchen'.[6] With the ability to make breakfast or a light meal in any

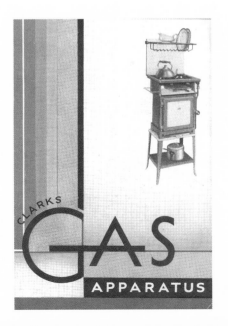

This 1930s brochure offers a range of gas appliances for the small home, including toasters and irons as well as stoves.
BADDA 398

Advertisement for a washing machine, 1930s.
BADDA 578

room with a power point, the servantless housewife was not necessarily confined to the kitchen.

Washing machines were still expensive and unsophisticated in design in the inter-war period. Many suburban women used laundries and local washer women for sheets, shirts and collars etc. The only change in clothes washing in the suburban home itself was in the increased availability of hot water via the boiler, although the electric iron did go some way towards alleviating this most laborious of household duties. As almost the cheapest of electrical appliances (selling at around fifteen shillings – 75p – in 1939), it replaced the heavy sad-iron which needed constant reheating on the hob. Its merits are evident in its popularity; by 1939, 77 percent of the homes wired for electricity owned an electric iron.[7]

The vacuum cleaner, although not as popular as the electric iron, provides possibly the best example of the commercialisation of cleanliness in the 1930s. Vacuum cleaners operated manually by servants had been in use for some years but developments in the electric vacuum cleaner ensured its wide availability for use in the servantless house of the new

suburbs. The price of this appliance fell considerably in the 1930s, due to changes in construction to cheaper and lighter materials. This made the machine easier to use but also more prone to damage and therefore replacement.

Manufacturers adopted 'hard sell' policies (the vacuum cleaner salesman plying his trade on the suburban street was the cause of much amusement) with catchy mottos such as Hoover Ltd's, 'it beats as it sweeps as it cleans'. The most significant feature of the appliance, however, was that it made possible more efficient cleaning with much less work; the housewife could use her latest acquisition without an apron and therefore without looking like a housemaid.

THE HOUSEWIFE

Manufacturers promoted the idea that because appliances were labour-saving, housework was something to be enjoyed. Laing, building new homes in North London, suggested 'women's work is turned into a pleasure in Laing's Deluxe Kitchen'.[8] Yet, despite the prestige attached to home ownership in the new suburbs, the housewife was more akin to the working-class woman of the 19th century than the middle-class woman whose housework had been done by servants. It thus became necessary to create a new image for household duties, which was undertaken largely by appliance manufacturers and in women's magazines. The latter were also quick to recognise the social status attached to women who worked after marriage; housework was now portrayed as a 'career', with *Good Housekeeping* referring to housewives as 'the craftworkers of today'. The kitchen became the 'domestic workshop' in which the professional housewife could execute her duties scientifically and efficiently with the help of labour-saving devices, all for the comfort of her family.

Books and manuals abounded with daily agendas for household tasks. *The Housewife's Book* even allowed time from 8.00pm for reading and recreation but suggested the housewife stopped at 8.40pm in order to do her accounts.[9] Estate developers were eager to exploit this image by offering free domestic equipment with the house; as one female resident of New Southgate in the 1930s recalled:

In the space-saving Laing's 'Deluxe Kitchen' the kitchen table could fold away when not in use. Brochure for Laing's Edgware Estate, 1936.
BADDA 688

'I was given an enamel-topped kitchen table and a choice of electric or gas cooker…other builders offered irons, electric bulbs and fittings, and tables with pop-up mangles.'

Emphasis on housework as a profession, however, had the disadvantage of demanding high standards from women, at the expense of other personal or social interests. They were now obliged to spend more time than ever before on more efficient housework; the British Electrical Development Association for example, proudly announced that electricity enabled 'Spring Cleanliness *Every Day*'. [10]

HYGIENE

The preoccupation with hygiene in the 'healthy' suburbs was not confined solely to the kitchen but justified changes in design throughout the house. Except in the more expensive suburban homes, where a daily maid might be employed, features such as panelled walls and doors were replaced by smoother, flatter and easier to clean surfaces.

Most household dust was caused by coal fires and was seen as the great harbourer of dirt and disease; yet coal fires remained for a long time the cheapest and most popular form of heating, despite the obvious labour-saving attributes of gas and electricity. However, by the mid-30s, suburban homes began to include fitted gas or wall-panel electric fires in the bedrooms. This meant that the household was not confined to one room in the evenings and at weekends. Not everyone took advantage of this facility and, for economy's sake, many preferred the cosy intimacy of the family sitting-room.

Its obvious associations with cleanliness meant that a plumbed-in bathroom suite and separate lavatory became standard in North London's suburban homes, built in the 20s and 30s. Possession of such was joy for those who were accustomed to a tin bath in front of the kitchen stove. The opulent bathrooms available to the wealthy at the turn of the century were now out of fashion; the hygienic revolution remodelled the bathroom on simple undecorated lines. However, by 1919, similar bathrooms were also being installed in London's council houses and so it became necessary to distinguish working-class from middle-class bathrooms by insisting on comfort as well as hygiene. Estate developers made much of this by advertising extras; the heated towel rail became a status symbol as did borders of geometrically patterned wall tiles, both streamlined to suggest cleanliness and compliance with the latest decorative fashion.

SHOPPING

If labour saving was the tenet of the time, so too was financial economy. The foundation was laid for the mass produced consumer goods market of the 1950s with the rapid expansion of chain stores such as Marks and Spencer. Wood Green for example boasted a Woolworth's selling nothing over 6d (six old pennies). In contrast, the parades of shops which followed the newly built houses in the suburbs could afford to be expensive

This fully tiled bathroom was standard in AW Curton's substantial houses in Edgware, 1939.
BADDA 312

because of their convenience. (This convenience perhaps explains why refrigerators were thought an unnecessary expenditure.) Moreover, these shops played an important social role: the shopping trip provided the pram-pushing housewife with an opportunity to exchange gossip and check that baby was as well turned out as her neighbour's.

As gardening was popular, money could be saved on home-grown vegetables but this did not stop the grocer's delivery van from disrupting the tranquillity of a suburban afternoon. Indeed, the baker, milkman and coalman with horse and cart, were also responsible for interrupting the low drone of the vacuum cleaner on the suburban air. Even wealthier areas like Winchmore Hill did not escape the attentions of the lesser tradesmen, or beggars who hoped to gain a penny for a cup of tea.

Despite the popularity of labour-saving appliances, the gadget-run home of today had no place in inter-war suburban life. The social forces which insisted that the woman's place was in the home could sometimes mean boredom and loneliness and rendered her little better off than her 19th-century, middle-class predecessor who was consigned to a life of leisure for the same status reasons.

For the suburban women in the 1920s and 30s, contradictions underlie the creation of her specific role as housewife and homemaker: in making a full-time profession out of housework, the concept of the labour-saving appliance was made redundant. In addition, in some cases, the lone housewife in the servantless home was forced to endure the day-long isolation of the very domestic sanctuary she herself created as the ideal suburban life.

Phillippa Mapes

LEISURE

The leisure, entertainment and tourist industries are big business today, with some of the largest corporations in the world involved. Part of the reason for their growth has been the decrease in working hours and a general increase in the disposable income of a large number of people. From the 1920s onwards, leisure became a more public activity with the popularity of cinemas, dance halls, spectator sports, libraries and restaurants. The 1920s and 1930s were also years when leisure was becoming dominated by the gramophone and mass media: press, radio and

Rug-making was a popular hobby, which also saved money. This picture is taken from Paton & Baldwin's Rugcraft, a 1930s booklet which illustrated a wide range of patterns and indicated the pleasures to be had when the rug was finished.
BADDA 166

The last knot is made; the binding has been sewn on, and after a final rub-down the new Turkey Rug has been laid in its proper place for the first time. What a thrill it is to see your handiwork come to a successful and beautiful result! Since it is made from Turkey Wool, you are sure that the rug is as hard-wearing as it is good-looking.

film. Even then there was concern that the commercialisation of leisure was making the nation more passive – listening to canned music instead of playing darts or singing round the piano in the pub, silently engrossed at the pictures instead of booing in the music halls.

For those who could afford them, the new suburban homes meant more space, greater comfort and privacy. These houses, complete with

garden, symbolised a 'touch of the country' but were not too far from the workplace in town. Despite the general trend to more public leisure pursuits, the majority of home owners, having come from cramped, inner-city accommodation, were only too happy to spend their leisure hours on predominantly home-based activities.

IN THE HOME

In photographs of interiors from the 20s and 30s, the piece of furniture which appears to take pride of place is the wireless. For most people it was the first piece of electrical equipment they owned. Costing the equivalent of two weeks' pay, many bought on hire purchase. Interest in radio increased rapidly. In 1922, when broadcasting began, there were 36,000 licences for receivers. By 1939, there were nine million, enough for almost every member of the population to have access to one.[1]

At first, wireless cabinets were designed to look like pieces of furniture but complaints from customers that their guests frequently mistook the set for the cocktail cabinet encouraged some manufacturers to rethink their ideas. Wireless sets of a more modern design promoted the idea that radio symbolised the future and represented everything that living rooms and lives lacked.

Broadcasters did what they could to make the experience of 'listening in' as real as possible and would suggest that people sit in a darkened room to 'listen in'. Creating the illusion of reality did on occasion cause confusion. A classic example was the occasion in the United States when Orson Welles' version of *War of the Worlds* by HG Wells was broadcast: 'Thousands of people who had turned on their sets during the programme fled from their homes, convinced that the Martian invasion was actually happening'.[2] Along with the BBC, whose programmes tended to be of a serious nature, there were commercial stations providing popular music and light entertainment. These were funded by advertising and sponsorship. The adverts were aimed predominantly at the middle-class suburban housewife, although children were not left out. By 1938, Radio Luxembourg's advert for Ovaltine had recruited one million 'Ovaltineys', drinking it every day. Programmes often centred on subjects connected with the home and garden, one of the most popular being Mr Middleton's gardening talks on the BBC.

Some of the estate developers were aware of the nuisance that this new technology might cause neighbours but they used it to their advantage. For example, Baldwin & Co advertised their £875 houses at Mill Hill (Thornfield Avenue) with the slogan, 'the next door wireless cannot be heard'.[3] For those tired of 'listening in' there were other popular pastimes: singing round the piano, playing the gramophone, or perhaps a game of cards or a board game with the rest of the family. Reading increased in popularity, with books borrowed rather than bought, perhaps coming from a local 'twopenny library' such as the one in Boots, the chemist's shop.

Just as the wireless edged the piano out of the living-room limelight, later the television took the place of the radio. Alexandra Palace started television transmission in 1937, although until the 1950s most people's experience of it was confined to the window of an electrical shop or the local cinema café.

There were few people who spent their spare time on do-it-yourself activities, although magazines such as The Woodworker were available. Newly built houses were often sold decorated and consequently needed little attention and, if necessary, the exterior of a medium-sized semi could be redecorated by a painter for £5 in the early 1930s. Do-it-yourself became a more popular leisure pursuit after 1945 due to a scarcity of outside labour.

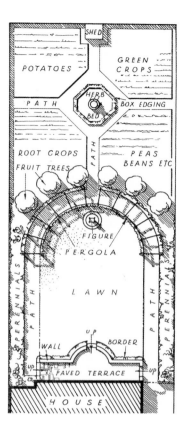

Plan for a back garden, with vegetables at the bottom. The vegetable area was often screened off by a trellis or pergola. The Ideal Home, January 1932.

THE GARDEN

The garden was of the greatest importance to most of the new homeowners, as for many it was the first time they had owned a piece of land. Gardening was a leisure activity that husbands and wives could undertake together and a creative outlet for residents whose working hours were probably spent indoors in an office or shop. It was quite usual to have gardening societies at the workplace which would organise shows and competitions. In addition, shows were put on by residents' associations or church societies.

Estate developers were aware of the difference a well-tended row of front gardens made on sales; some put on competitions for the best-looking garden whilst houses remained unsold: 'At Cannons Park in 1935

O-C Estates presented a cash prize of £15 (five times the average weekly wage) and a challenge cup to the winner of a front garden competition'.[4]

The front garden, with its privet hedges, separated the house from the street and was usually larger than those found in many Edwardian and later Victorian suburbs. The hedge might be 'topped with iron chains – which was suggestive perhaps of the drawbridge and castle wall'.[5] The back garden was more private with a fence or wall down each side. Even so, many occupants wanted more seclusion and raised the low walls or fences erected by the builder to as high as eight feet. Part of the back garden was often used for growing vegetables but the half nearest the house would

A local bee-keeping society in about 1934.
Photograph courtesy of London Borough of Enfield.

Swimming was another popular outdoor activity. These are the new baths at Harrow in the early 1930s.
BADDA 439

usually be taken up by a lawn, edged by neat flowers beds, perhaps with a crazy paving path and a rockery. Ornaments for the garden were popular and it was not unusual to see 'concrete bird baths and those red plaster elves you can buy at the florist's'.[6]

SOCIAL ACTIVITIES

On both the private estates and those built by the London County Council it could take a few years before shops, parks, libraries and other local amenities were built. Hendon, with a population of 134,000, did not get its first branch library until 1935. The lack of facilities meant residents were forced to entertain themselves. Most estates had a residents' or ratepayers' association, often started by the builder or developer. It was through these local associations that a variety of societies were set up. For example, the Edgware Literary Society was started up in 1926 and was still active in 1939. There was also the Edgware Dramatic Group, which was formed in 1927 and based at the Express Dairy Hall. The group shared this hall with the Operatic Society and held regular Saturday night dances from June 1935. Evening classes and dance classes were well attended; popular dances such as the Charleston, Foxtrot and Tango had intricate steps and required practice. The dance of the period that gripped all classes was the 'Lambeth Walk', introduced in 1938 by the West End show, *Me and My Girl*.

In the 1930s, people became obsessed with fresh air and healthy exercise, so tennis and cricket clubs flourished on many estates. In 1931, Edgware boasted three tennis courts, all of which were private. Golf clubs were confined to the wealthier suburbs only. On Saturday afternoons the men in the family might watch their favourite football team play at White Hart Lane or go greyhound racing at Hendon Stadium, built in 1934.

Few people in the new suburbs owned cars in the 1920s but by the outbreak of the Second World War this was changing. In 1931 there were one million private cars on the road; less than one family in ten owned one. However, for those fortunate enough to have access to a car, Sunday afternoons became popular for motoring to the seaside or a recognised beauty spot. This activity was frowned upon by the religious as Sunday was traditionally a day to attend church, both morning and evening, with afternoon Sunday school for children.

CINEMA

The cinema was probably the most popular form of entertainment outside the home and one that had a profound influence on people's lives. The number of cinemas escalated dramatically in the thirty years from 1910; in 1912 the London Evening News recorded that there were some 500 cinemas open in London and its suburbs. By 1934 there were eighteen and a half million admissions which had risen to twenty-two million by 1939.

No suburb was without its 'modern cathedral' and in 1928 the Lido at Golders Green was the first of the suburban super-cinemas to be equipped for sound. It was designed by WJ King, had seating for 1,959, a Christie-Unit organ, a café lounge and parking space for one hundred cars. The Ionic, another cinema in Golders Green, was described as 'a perfect

example of a classical 'pomp' front grafted onto a plain brick box-like
hall,…and rows of tiny boxes along the sides, evidently designed for privacy
rather than any possibility of seeing more than one corner of the screen.'[7]
Other North London cinemas included the Ritz (Edgware), the Astoria
(Finsbury Park), the Odeon (Muswell Hill) and the Burnt Oak Regent.

Eighty percent of the films shown in these cinemas were made in
Hollywood and helped to promote American culture and products. But there
were British films around, such as *The Good Companions* (1932) starring John
Gielgud and Jessie Matthews, *Sing As We Go* (1934) with Gracie Fields and

Keep Your Seats Please (1936) with George Formby, to name a few. British filmgoers loved such stars as Greta Garbo, Charles Boyer and Marlene Dietrich, who were glamorously remote with their foreign accents and exotic names. Films also influenced fashion and, to a lesser extent, interior decoration as explained in *The New Survey of London Life and Labour* (1934):

> Girls copy the fashions of their favourite film star. At the time of writing, girls in all classes of society wear 'Garbo' coats and wave their hair à la Norma Shearer and Lillian Harvey. It is impossible to measure the effect that films must have on the outlook and habits of the people.

To enter these palaces of wish fulfillment and escapism cost as little as 6d (six old pennies), which matched the cheapest music hall of the day. Even Gordon Comstock, a character in George Orwell's *Keep the Aspidistra Flying*, recognised their attraction:

> …Greta Garbo in *Painted Veil*. He yearned to go inside, not for Greta's sake but just for warmth and the softness of the velvet seat. He hated the pictures… But still, there is a kind of soggy attraction about it. To sit on the padded seat in the warm smoke-scented darkness, letting the flickering drivel on the screen gradually overwhelm you. [8]

The interior was given as much attention as the neon-lit exterior of the cinema; the decoration was influenced by Egyptian and Mexican symbolism, or loud geometric patterns. A trip to one of the West End cinemas would have been slightly more expensive, with plusher interiors and luxurious powder- rooms for the ladies. The theatre and music hall declined in popularity in the 30s often being turned into cinemas, although most cinemas put on cine-variety shows until at least 1945. The most successful plays at the time tended to be light romantic or society comedies such as Noel Coward's *Private Lives* and his spectacular musical, *Cavalcade*, with a cast of 400.

HOLIDAYS

By the end of the 1930s, half of the families in Britain took at least one holiday a year, travelling by train to such resorts as Watergate Bay in Devon, Bournemouth, Margate and Clacton. More people now had paid holidays; civil servants, for instance, received one week's holiday a year.

Hiking and rambling had become the great outdoor sports of the period. The Underground Group published two guide books in 1923. Hikers were numerous and railway companies ran special hiking trains which went on mystery tours into the countryside. At least ten million people owned

The London and North Eastern Railway (LNER) served the east coast resorts right up to Scotland. Advertisement in The Ideal Home, April 1939.

a bicycle in the 1930s; a new Raleigh cost £5 in 1932 and a Hercules less than £4. In the summer, roads would be full of groups of cyclists on weekend expeditions with their local cycling club. One week's holiday 'all in' would cost £3.10s (£3.50p) in cyclists' touring club accommodation or even less at the Youth Hostel Association, which had 93,000 members by 1939.

Holiday camps came into existence in the 1930s. Billy Butlin opened his first camp at Skegness in 1937 and by 1939 there were 100 Butlin camps. They were usually situated near the sea or by a funfair and consisted of wooden huts surrounding communal dining-rooms and games-rooms. Everything from meals to entertainment was provided for the whole family.

By the late 1930s the world cruise, popular earlier in the period, was less in demand, as many of the rich had fallen on hard times. Instead, Cunard started running short cruises lasting a few weeks, visiting ports around the Mediterranean and the Canaries. These cruises and other cut-price package deals across the Channel meant the English could now go in search of a suntan.

The number of workers employed by the entertainment and sports industries increased from 65,000 in 1930 to 116,000 in 1937 and it was the middle classes who were able to enjoy the new consumer revolution, the England of, '…arterial and by-pass roads, or filling stations and factories that look like exhibition buildings, of giant cinemas and dance halls and cafes, bungalows with tiny garages, cocktail bars, Woolworths, motor coaches, wireless, hiking, factory girls looking like actresses, greyhound racing and dirt tracks, swimming pools and everything given away for cigarette coupons.'[9]

Sue Andrew

TRANSPORT

On the eve of the First World War, North London already possessed a varied and sophisticated public transport system that had developed over the preceding 65 years. From the mid 19th century, steam services of the Midland Railway had run from St Pancras via Hendon to St Albans and beyond. From Liverpool Street, the Great Eastern Railway served Alexandra Palace, Waltham Cross and Enfield. Between these two, the

Escalators and pedestal lights at Southgate station in about 1933.

Great Northern Railway had developed, from 1846, an extensive suburban network. Lines from Edgware, Alexandra Palace, two Barnet stations and Enfield all converged on an inadequate bottleneck at Finsbury Park, where the great numbers of trains and passengers frequently created chaotic scenes.

The early 20th century had brought important changes, with fast electric trams run by Metropolitan Electric Tramways (MET) replacing horsepower after 1905 and electric underground railway lines from Central London opening at Golders Green, Highgate and Finsbury Park by 1908. These lines, fed by MET trams from Finchley, Barnet and Tottenham (and with the possibility of through-booking from 1914), significantly cut both journey times and the income of the railway companies. Motor buses had also been introduced in this period but only really became a force to be reckoned with when the London General Omnibus Company (LGOC) introduced its famous B Type bus in October 1910. By 1915 horse-drawn public transport had effectively ceased to exist.

The 19th-century railways had encouraged suburban growth considerably. Along some lines, such as the Great Northern main line through New Barnet, a ribbon of housing had already spread as far as the present Green Belt by 1914. The MET trams stimulated more growth and led to significant development at Palmers Green, Winchmore Hill, Southgate and Enfield, the last-named growing by 32 percent from 1900 – 1911.[1] The Underground, however, did not really penetrate the suburbs before the 20s except at Golders Green, where it played a very important role. Both Golders Green itself and places served by trams feeding the station grew swiftly, Finchley for example increasing its population by 78 percent from 1901 – 1911.[2] The First World War marked a lull rather than a watershed in London's transport history. The quality of services suffered in the war but little change occurred. Even the introduction of conductresses due to manpower shortages was short-lived and men took back most of these jobs when peace came. The important developments had taken place in the decade before the war and in the 20s the time was right to capitalise on them.

THE TWENTIES

Wartime conditions gave the railways, already losing out in competition with the trams, a very poor reputation for reliability. All the companies attempted to rationalise their services. The Great Eastern was the most successful in this respect. It spent £70,000 creating its much-publicised 'Jazz

Golders Green station in 1924.
Most of the buses are
of the K type.

Traffic on the Finchley Road at Golders Green, 1927. Almost every type of road transport can be seen. Photograph courtesy of London's Transport Museum.

Service', introduced in July 1920 and so named because of the yellow and blue bands indicating first and second class.[3]

Such reforms delayed electrification by decades and thus saved much money in the short term, but they failed to revitalise the suburban railways which changed little between the wars. The number of motor buses had increased dramatically from 1911 but the war had ended production and many B Types had been requisitioned in France. When peace came there was a shortage of motor buses; army lorries, hastily fitted with seats, had to be drafted in as auxiliaries. In August 1919, the K Type bus was introduced, seating more than the B Type and marking the final rejection of horse bus design but significant numbers of motor buses did not become available until 1922. When they did, they marked the beginning of fierce competition for the LGOC. By 1914 most London passenger transport, including the LGOC and MET, was controlled by the Underground group, commonly known as the Combine. This made sense, especially since in 1919 a select committee reported that there was too much unnecessary competition in public transport but the Combine was unpopular because of high fares (1d per mile) and poor service inherited from the war.[4] From 1922 many independent bus companies were founded, sometimes by ex-officers using gratuities and employing men who had gained mechanical experience in the army. Although perfectly legal these were often known as 'pirates'.

Many pirates ran at peak times only, taking passengers from the LGOC's most profitable routes. Some of the disreputable crews would carry several destination boards and change course if they saw richer pickings across the street. For their part LGOC buses would chase pirate vehicles and developed a technique called 'nursing', designed to block off a rival bus from its passengers. Both sides probably indulged in this dangerous practice. Although some people admired the little man's struggle against the Combine and small boys doubtless enjoyed watching the gaily-coloured private buses, most people were worried by the sight of four-ton omnibuses racing each other along increasingly busy streets.

The 1924 Road Traffic Act reflected this by regulating bus services. Unregulated competition is illogical in a great city and the nature of the pirates generally prevented their co-operating with each other. This, together with the 1924 Act, greatly favoured the LGOC and by 1930 few of the pirates were left; some went bankrupt and many were absorbed by the Combine. However, this episode had probably stimulated major bus design, already developing swiftly because of competition with non-Combine London County Council trams. By 1923 the new NS Type bus was introduced, a low-loading vehicle which over the next seven years acquired a covered roof, pneumatic tyres and an enclosed driver's cab and could be described as the first modern bus. 1923 was also the year when buses for the first time carried more passengers than did trams.

It was however to be the underground railway that provided the real stimulus to suburban growth in the inter-war years. 1919 marked a major watershed with the introduction of the first air-operated sliding doors. But the important change for North London came in the early 1920s with the extension of the line from Golders Green to Edgware, with services to Hendon Central beginning in November 1923 and to Edgware itself in August 1924. Although significant development had already occurred as far out as Hendon through the influence of trams, and although in the first two years of operation the line only showed a 14 percent increase in passengers, the overall effect cannot be over-stressed.

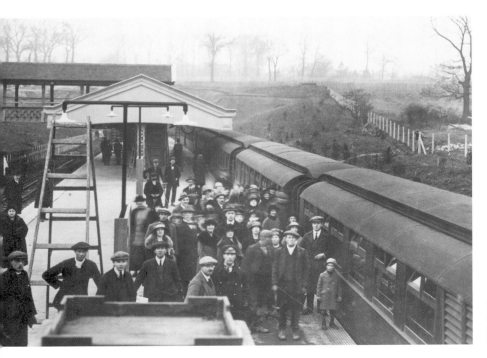

The first train from Hendon Central, November 1923. Photograph courtesy of London's Transport Museum.

INLAND REVENUE

PICCADILLY RAILWAY
SOUTHGATE EXTENSION FROM FINSBURY PARK

UNDERGROUND **ENFIELD WEST STATION SITE**

CHASE ROAD

The Piccadilly line was extended from Arnos Grove to Cockfosters in 1932 and 1933, opening the area for development. Enfield West later became Oakwood. Photograph courtesy of London Borough of Enfield.

In 1921 Edgware was a small village. By the early 1930s it was a suburb thirty-five minutes from Central London, with a train every five minutes. Hendon's total population rose from 57,566 in 1921 to 115,640 in 1931 and reached 146,000 by the war.[5] In 1929 two million people used the stations north of Brent in a single month and by the mid-30s the line was the busiest in London.[6]

THE THIRTIES

The Edgware extension's enormous impetus to suburban development in the west of the area was to be balanced nearly ten years later by another underground project, the Piccadilly extension from Finsbury Park to Cockfosters. In 1925, a Ministry of Transport commission suggested that such a line would relieve congestion in North London, especially at the still beleaguered Finsbury Park, since 1923 under the control of the London &

North Eastern Railway (LNER). The Great Northern had held a veto on any underground extension but the LNER now withdrew this obstruction and a line was planned running under Green Lanes and then out into the country to Cockfosters, the only place with adequate space for a depot.

As in the case of the Edgware line, some of this area had already been developed but much new building was a direct result of the arrival of the railway. Work began in autumn 1930 and the line was opened in stages from September 1932 (Arnos Grove) to July 1933 (Cockfosters). It was equipped with the very latest rolling stock. On the Edgware extension the Underground Group had engaged their own architect, SA Heaps, to build Italianate 'London Electric Doric' station buildings in keeping with the rural

The newly opened Cockfosters station in 1933.
Photograph courtesy of London's Transport Museum.

surroundings. But for the Piccadilly Line Charles Holden was commissioned to build striking modern structures strongly influenced by the North European architecture that he had visited in 1930 with Frank Pick, Managing Director of the Underground Group. Under Pick's enlightened leadership the Underground was at the forefront of modern design in the 1930s and the Piccadilly extension stations are some of the best new commercial architecture of the period.

The public was invited to choose the name for each new Piccadilly line station from a choice displayed on hoardings. Soon builders' publicity material was describing Southgate, where a large modern shopping complex was built around the station, as 'an area which, since the extension of the underground railway, has rapidly developed into a modern suburb'.[7] Such material also stressed the good value of underground season tickets – a quarterly season from Enfield West (now Oakwood) to Oxford Circus cost £3. 15s, (£3.75p) an average of about 10d (about 4p) a day. As with the Edgware branch, there was a slow start to passenger traffic but within three years the line was seriously poaching from the LNER. East Barnet, in the catchment area of some of the stations, rose in population from 18,549 in 1931 to 34,480 in 1939.[8] The Piccadilly extension was without doubt the direct cause of the 1930s building boom in the strip between seven and nine miles north of Kings Cross.

In 1933 all public transport in London, except for the surface railways, was brought under the London Passenger Transport Board (LPTB), a process already largely achieved by the Combine. In North London everything that mattered had been under unified control since before the First World War, except for LCC trams running through on MET track and the only obvious change was the new, gold London Transport lettering on the sides of the vehicles. During the 30s bus design continued to improve.

Enclosed staircases were introduced on the ST and LT Types, and the later LTs were also the first buses to have diesel engines and pre-selector transmission. The standard 1930s London bus was the STL Type, most of which incorporated all of these features. In 1939 the RT Type was introduced. This was to form the mainstay of London Transport's post-war fleet, and remained in service for forty years. From 1930 onwards North Londoners could also travel on Green Line coaches for excursions into the countryside.

Southgate underground station, with its striking circular entrance and booking hall, designed by Charles Holden. Photograph courtesy of London Borough of Enfield.

REFERENCES

INTRODUCTION

1 Semi-detached London – Jackson Alan A, 1973, p104

ARCHITECTURE

1 On the Garden Cities – Trevelyan CG, from *Red Rags, Essays of Hate From Oxford* – Carr RC (ed), 1933

2 Architectural Association Journal – November 1933

3 Journal of the Royal Institute of British Architects – 28 April 1934

4 Design – Bertram Anthony, p58, 1938

5 The Story of Haymills 1911-1975 – Cox DA, nd (typescript)

HOUSEHOLD MANAGEMENT

1 The Making of Modern London, 1914-1939 – Weightman G and Humphries S, 1984, p122. The national figure for the professional class rose from 744,000 persons in 1911 to 1,500,000 persons in 1921

2 Women's Magazines 1693 -1968 – White CL, 1970, pp100-101

3 Home in the Twenties and Thirties – Ward M and N, 1978, p43

4 The Electric Home – Forty A, from *History of Architecture and Design 1890-1939*, 1975, p41

5 Ibid p41

6 Belling & Company Ltd, publicity material, – c1930

7 The Making of Modern London, op cit, p131

8 John Laing Construction Ltd, publicity material – c1935

9 The Housewife's Book – c1925, p20

10 The Appliance of Science: Technology and Housework – Arnold E, from *New Scientist* 18 April 1985, p14

LEISURE

1 Objects of Desire – Forty A, 1986, p200

2 Ibid, p202

3 Semi-detached London – Jackson AA, 1973 p181

4 Ibid, p211

5 The Making of Modern London 1914-1939 – Weightman G and Humphries S, 1984, p141

6 Coming Up for Air – Orwell G, 1939

7 Cathedrals of the Movies: History of the British Cinemas and Their Audience – Atwell D, 1981

8 Keep the Aspidistra Flying – Orwell G, 1939

9 English Journey – Priestley JB, 1934

TRANSPORT

1 Semi-detached London – Jackson AA, 1973, p37

2 Ibid, p38

3 A History of London Transport, Vol 2 – Baker TC and Robbins M, 1974, p232

4 Ibid, p257

5 Semi-detached London, op cit, p326

6 Ibid, p239

7 George Reed & Sons Ltd, publicity material, Hornsey 1936, p9

8 Semi-detached London, op cit, p326

9 Great Northern Suburban – Young NJ, 1977, p70

10 The Expanding City – Freeborn J et al, 1986, p35

11 British Society 1914-1945 – Stevenson J, 1984, p390

SELECTED READING

Suburban Style. The British Home, 1840-1960 –
Barrett H and Phillips J, Macdonald, 1987
*Semi-detached London. Suburban development,
life and transport, 1900-39* – Jackson AA,
Allen and Unwin, 1973
Dunroamin: the suburban semi and its enemies
– Oliver P, Davis I and Bentley I, Barrie &
Jenkins, 1981
The 1930s Home – Stevenson G, Shire, 2000
Something in Linoleum, – Vaughan P, Sinclair-
Stevenson, 1994

ACKNOWLEDGEMENTS

The first edition of Little Palaces was published in 1987 by Middlesex Polytechnic (now Middlesex University). It accompanied an exhibition of the same name put on by the Silver Studio Collection, now incorporated into Middlesex University's Museum of Domestic Design & Architecture (MoDA).

Thanks are due to the many organisations and individuals who contributed to and supported the original *Little Palaces*, but especially to Miss Mary Peerless who donated the Silver Studio Collection, to the London Borough of Enfield whose Community Programme Scheme funded the exhibition team, and to the John Lewis Partnership for its generous sponsorship. Mark Turner, Keeper of the Silver Studio Collection, led the project team: Sue Andrew, Malcolm Barres-Baker, Malcolm Boyd, Phillippa Mapes and Mark Pinney.

For this edition, Oliver Green of London's Transport Museum was good enough to update the chapter on Transport. Apart from that, there are few changes to the original text but new illustrations have been introduced. Institutions which have kindly allowed the reproduction of images are: London's Transport Museum, the London Borough of Enfield and English Heritage (NMR). Unless otherwise credited, other images are from MoDA's own collections.

MoDA is known as the 'museum of the history of the home'. Its varied exhibitions give a vivid picture of domestic life during the first half of the twentieth century whilst also looking at contemporary design and other issues related to the domestic environment.

Gallery talks, events, practical workshops, and study days provide educational, informative and entertaining experiences for adults and children.

MoDA holds six collections and a dedicated Study Room allows access to items not on display.

SILVER STUDIO COLLECTION

The archive of a commercial pattern design practice active between 1880 and 1963. Its many thousands of designs, wallpapers and textile samples span the popular styles of the period.

CROWN WALLPAPER COLLECTION

Wallpaper books mainly from the 1950s, represent the colourful and engaging patterns of that time.

DOMESTIC DESIGN COLLECTION

More than 4,000 books, magazines and trade catalogues relating to design for the home and household management (1850-1960).

SIR JM RICHARDS LIBRARY

Books and journals collected by Sir JM Richards (1907-1992) a leading architectural writer. The collection covers architecture, interiors, furniture, landscape and town planning.

PEGGY ANGUS ARCHIVE

The entire contents of the London studio of Peggy Angus (1904-1993), an artist, teacher and designer of tiles and bespoke hand-printed wallpapers.

CHARLES HASLER COLLECTION

An archive relating to the work of Charles Hasler (1908-1992), a typographer and graphic designer who played a significant role in many high-profile exhibitions, poster campaigns and in book publishing from the mid-1930s to the mid-1980s.